Computers

Experts on child reading levels
have consulted on the level of text and
concepts in this book.

At the end of the book is a "Look Back and Find" section
which provides additional information and encourages
the child to refer back to previous pages
for the answers to the questions posed.

Angela Grunsell trained as a teacher in 1969.
She has a Diploma in Reading and Related Skills
and for the last five years has advised London
teachers on materials and resources.
She works for the ILEA as an advisory teacher in
primary schools in Hackney, London.

Published in the United States in 1984 by
Franklin Watts, 387 Park Avenue South, New York, NY 10016

© Aladdin Books Ltd/Franklin Watts

Designed and produced by
Aladdin Books Ltd, 70 Old Compton Street, London W1

ISBN 0 531 04810 1

Library of Congress Catalog Card Number 84 50602

Printed in Belgium

FRANKLIN · WATTS · FIRST · LIBRARY

Computers

by
Kate Petty

Consultant
Angela Grunsell

Illustrated by
Anthony Kerins

Franklin Watts
New York · London · Toronto · Sydney

Have you ever used a computer?
This little computer is called a micro.
There might be one like it at school or at home.

The keyboard looks like a typewriter.
Underneath the keyboard are the microchips
that do the work of the computer.

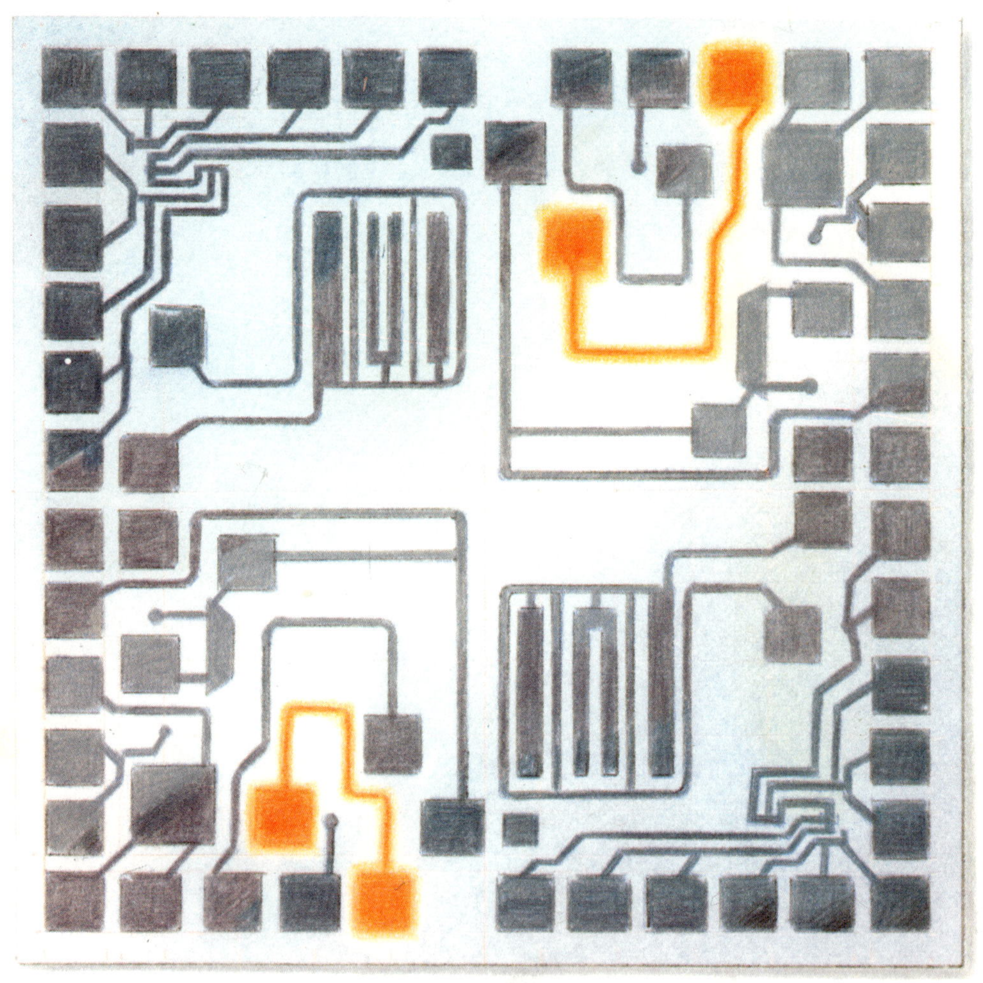

A computer is a machine that runs on electricity.
You tell it what to do by pressing the keys.
Then electrical messages can pass along the tiny
lines on the microchips. They look like this.

You need a screen to be able to see
what the computer is doing.
This micro can be connected to your TV.

Take a closer look at the keyboard. There are
words and signs as well as letters and numbers.
Can you find the key that says RETURN?

10

You can tell this computer to print your name.
Type it out and your name will
come up on the screen.

Computers can work with numbers
very quickly. The micro will do a sum
for you. The answer comes up on
the screen instantly.

The computer has a memory. On one
tiny memory chip it can store information
that would fill four books like this one.

So far you have given the computer
one instruction at a time. But it can
remember a whole list of instructions.
This is called a program.

Each step in the program has a number.
Then the computer can carry out the instructions
in the right order. You must not forget
to tell it when to stop.

Imagine that the screen is divided into lots
of tiny squares. Each square is called a pixel.
You can program the computer to make
a picture by filling in some of these pixels.

You can make different colors
by pressing the top row of keys.

This program is telling the computer
to play a tune. It can make other noises too.
The sound comes through a speaker on the side.
Now you have all you need to make up a game.

You can buy ready-made programs for games.
Games for computers come on disks, cartridges
or cassettes. All of these are called software.

This micro uses a cassette player.
It is connected to the computer.
As the tape runs the program is fed
directly into the computer.

You use the keyboard for playing the game.
Any instructions you need will appear
on the screen. This happens with disks and
cartridges too.

This game is helping a little girl at school
with her sums. The colored cardboard
laid over the keyboard makes it easier
for her to find the right keys.

The boys playing this game are
using a joystick to move
the battleships around.

23

This toy tank is a computer. You press the keys
to make it go left, right or straight ahead.
It can drive itself around the room.

The "turtle" is like a robot
attached to a microcomputer.
It will move in the direction you tell
it to go. As it moves it draws a picture.

People use computers of all sizes in their work.
You find them in hospitals, supermarkets,
libraries and airports, schools and offices.
All of them have been programmed to do a job.

You can have fun learning to write programs.
Many children join a club and share their ideas.
It is very exciting to be able to understand
these machines that are changing our lives.

Look back and find

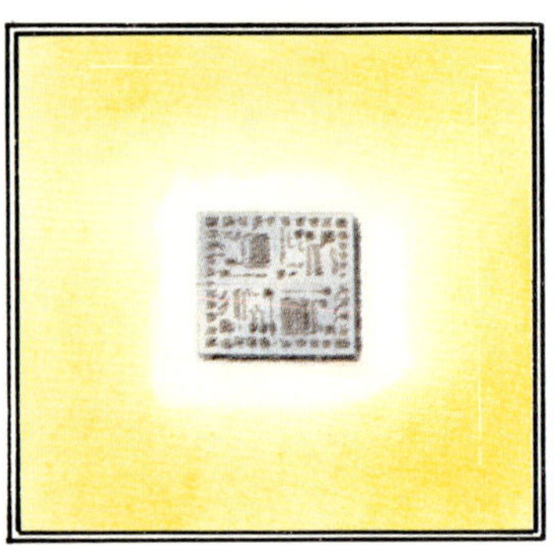

What must you do to start the computer working?
You must switch on the electric power.

What is the real size of a microchip?

How many chips are needed to do the
work of a micro?
Most micros contain about 15 chips.

Can you find the letters of your name
on the keyboard in the picture?

How would you make the spaces between
the words?
You press the bar at the bottom.

What is the proper name for a computer's screen?
A VDU, which stands for Visual Display Unit.

Why is the program in a special language?
*A machine only understands two things —
on (1) and off (0). Words and numbers
in machine code look like this — 00111010.
A computer has a built-in program to
translate just a few words into machine
code for itself. These are the words
you use to write programs.*

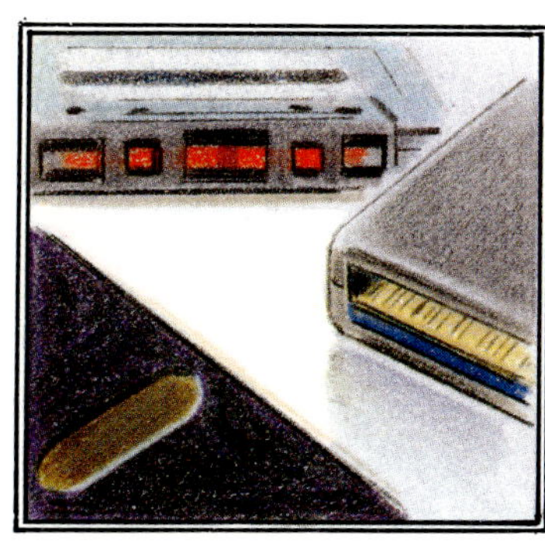

What sort of computer software have you used?

How are the programs on disks and cartridges fed into the computer?
Disks are slotted into a disk drive. Cartridges are plugged into the computer itself.

Have you played with any other computer toy?

What was it called?

What did it do?

How is the librarian using a computer?
The "magic" pen records the code on your ticket and on the book.
The information is stored on a computer.

Where else do you see bar codes like the one on your ticket?
On items bought in supermarkets.

PRINTED IN BELGIUM BY
proost
INTERNATIONAL BOOK PRODUCTION